SIMPLE SIGNS

Cindy Wheeler

SCHOLASTIC INC.

New York   Toronto   London   Auckland   Sydney

To my son, Will

ISBN 0-590-88020-9

Copyright © 1995 by Cindy Wheeler.
All rights reserved. Published by Scholastic Inc., 555 Broadway, New York, NY 10012, by arrangement with Penguin Books USA Inc.

12 11 10 9 8 7 6 5 4   2/0

Printed in the U.S.A.   08

First Scholastic printing, January 1997

Author's Note

My son, Will, was born with Down Syndrome. As is typical of such kids, Will's speech came very slowly, and when he was about one year old his speech therapist began teaching him American Sign Language (ASL). By the time Will was eighteen months old, he knew how to sign that he wanted to "eat" or "sleep." He was able to sign that he wanted "more" or that he was "finished." And he could sign that he loved me.

As my daughter, my husband, and I learned ASL with Will, we became impressed with the beauty—and the simplicity—of the signs. Some children learn to sign the alphabet when they reach school age. But word-signs are accessible even to preschoolers who do not yet know the alphabet. The appeal is much the same as that of finger plays such as "Eentsy-Weentsy Spider." The benefits are without number.

Simple Signs is my tribute to the language that let me communicate with my son.

If you would like to know more about ASL, here are some of the resources I used in preparing this book:

Benjamin Bahan, Joe Dannis, and Frank Paul. *Signs for Me: A Basic Sign Language for Children, Parents & Teachers.* Dawn Sign Press, 1987.

Elaine Costello. *Random House American Sign Language Dictionary.* Random House, Inc., 1994.

Lottie Riekehof. *The Joy of Signing.* Gospel Publishing House, 1987.

hello

hint: like saluting

hint: show a cat's whiskers

cat

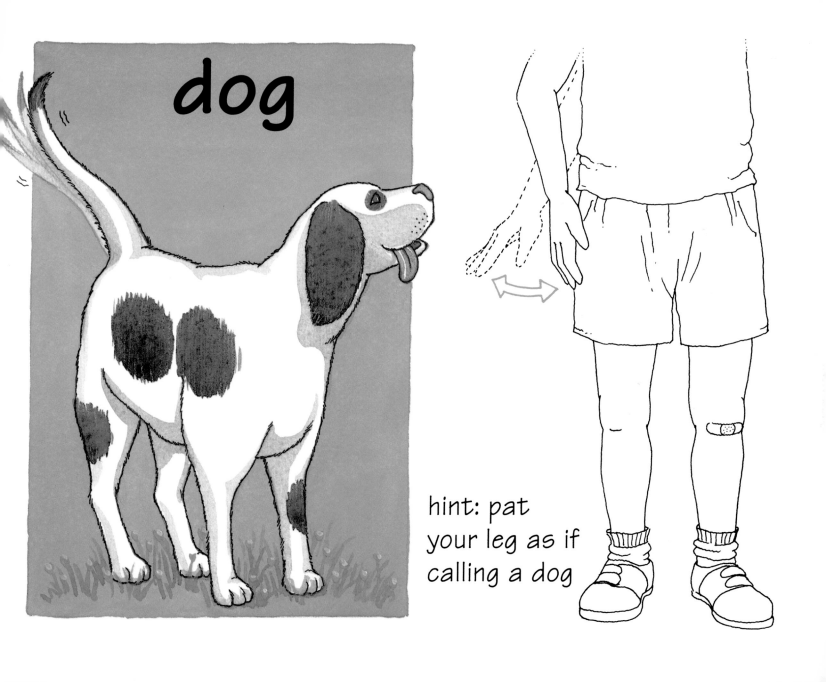

dog

hint: pat your leg as if calling a dog

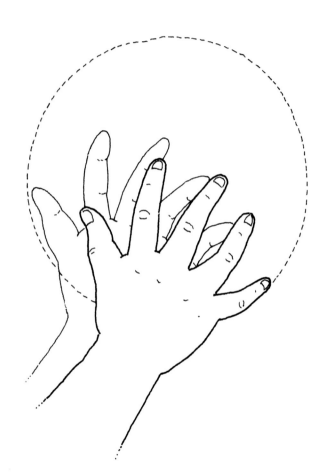

hint: like holding a ball

ball

car

hint: like driving a car

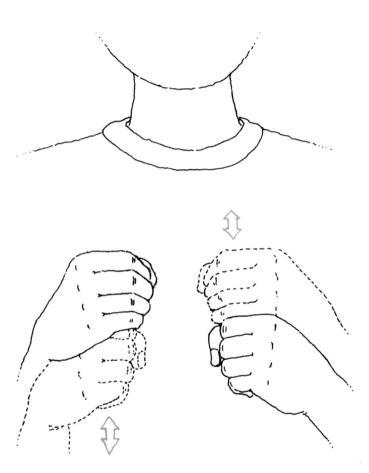

hint: like milking a cow

milk

banana

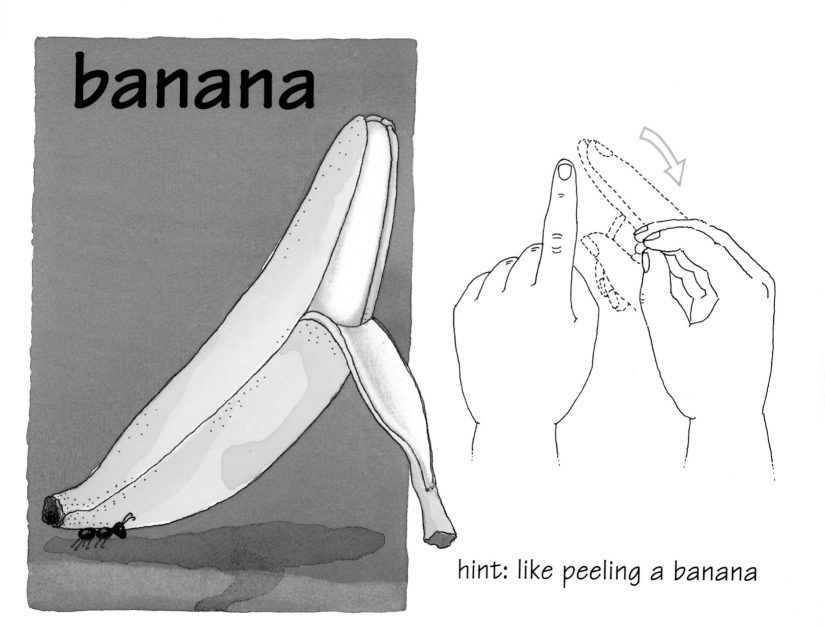

hint: like peeling a banana

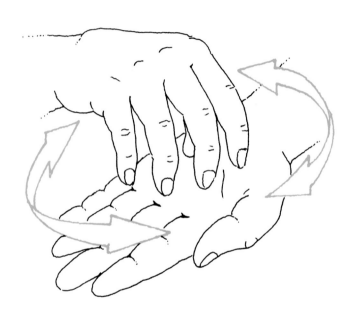

hint: like using a
cookie cutter

cookie

eat

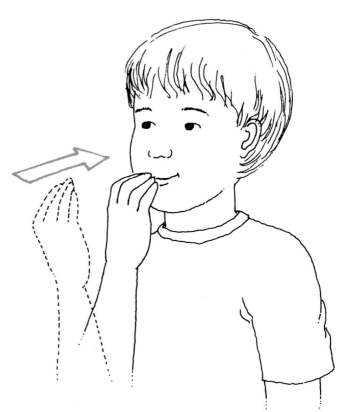

hint: like putting food
in your mouth

hint: touch fingertips
together

more

finished

hint: like brushing crumbs
off your shirt

hint: make a loop up
from your heart

happy

cry

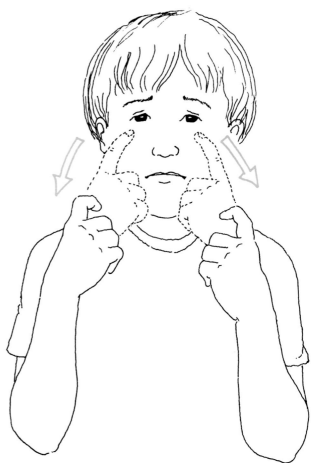

hint: show falling tears
with fingertips

1.

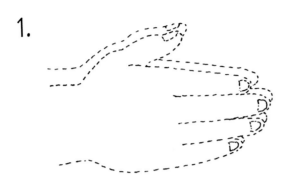

2.

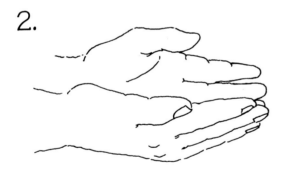

hint: like opening
a book

book

music

hint: like
conducting music

hint: like rocking a baby

baby

mother & father

mother
hint:
thumb
on
chin

father
hint:
thumb
on forehead

bird

hint: fingers open and
close like a bird's beak

COW

hint: stick out little finger
like a cow's horn and
wag it up and down

hint: like a butterfly's
wings fluttering

butterfly

turtle

hint: curve top hand like
a shell, wiggle thumb
like a turtle's head

snake

hint: shape fingers
like fangs, move
hands like a snake

elephant

hint: show
an elephant's trunk

1.

2.

hint: index fingers hook
one way then the other

friend

bicycle

hint: like pedaling
a bicycle

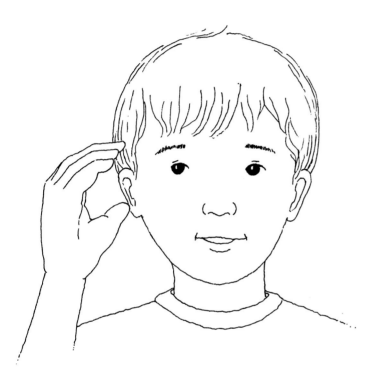

hint: make hand
into a C-shape like
a crescent moon

moon

sleep

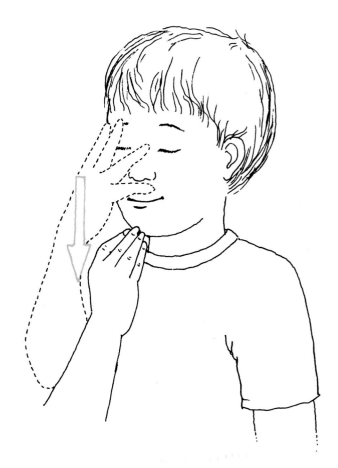

hint: like eyes
being closed

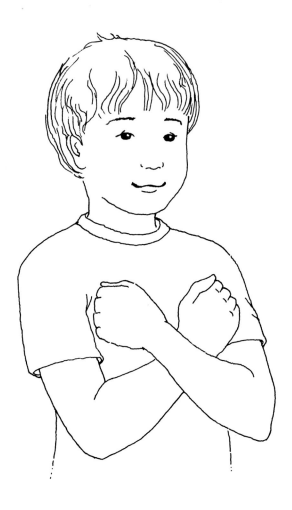

hint: like a hug

love